ISBN 978-1-332-61278-9
PIBN 10219827

This book is a reproduction of an important historical work. Forgotten Books uses state-of-the-art technology to digitally reconstruct the work, preserving the original format whilst repairing imperfections present in the aged copy. In rare cases, an imperfection in the original, such as a blemish or missing page, may be replicated in our edition. We do, however, repair the vast majority of imperfections successfully; any imperfections that remain are intentionally left to preserve the state of such historical works.

1 MONTH OF FREE READING

at
www.ForgottenBooks.com

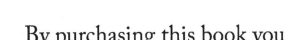

By purchasing this book you are eligible for one month membership to ForgottenBooks.com, giving you unlimited access to our entire collection of over 1,000,000 titles via our web site and mobile apps.

To claim your free month visit:

www.forgottenbooks.com/free219827

English
Français
Deutsche
Italiano
Español
Português

www.forgottenbooks.com

Mythology Photography **Fiction**
Fishing Christianity **Art** Cooking
Essays Buddhism Freemasonry
Medicine **Biology** Music **Ancient**
Egypt Evolution Carpentry Physics
Dance Geology **Mathematics** Fitness
Shakespeare **Folklore** Yoga Marketing
Confidence Immortality Biographies
Poetry **Psychology** Witchcraft
Electronics Chemistry History **Law**
Accounting **Philosophy** Anthropology
Alchemy Drama Quantum Mechanics
Atheism Sexual Health **Ancient History**
Entrepreneurship Languages Sport
Paleontology Needlework Islam
Metaphysics Investment Archaeology
Parenting Statistics Criminology
Motivational

the Creeds as containing the one unchangeable Faith of Christ,—and a blessing shall be poured out upon it from on high. It shall "lengthen its cords and strengthen its stakes, burst forth on the right hand and on the left," and even yet, through the mighty power and indwelling of the Spirit of God, become a praise upon earth.

A

PASTORAL LETTER

TO

THE CLERGY AND LAITY OF THE PROVINCE OF YORK.

BY

WILLIAM LORD ARCHBISHOP OF YORK,

PRIMATE OF ENGLAND AND METROPOLITAN.

LONDON:
JOHN MURRAY, ALBEMARLE STREET.
1864.

LONDON : PRINTED BY WILLIAM CLOWES AND SONS, STAMFORD STREET,

TO THE CLERGY AND LAITY OF THE PROVINCE OF YORK.

Brethren,

The result of the proceedings before the Privy Council, in the two cases of the *Bishop of Salisbury* v. *Williams* and *Fendall* v. *Wilson*, has caused great perplexity and dismay throughout the Church. The numerous addresses and letters which have reached me, inviting an expression of opinion upon the great questions supposed to be involved, seem to compel me to some public and general reply, in order to remove misapprehensions, and to reassure, it may be, the minds of some, who have admitted, in their first alarm, the notion that the Church of England is falling away from the true faith.

My position, as a member of the Privy Council, necessarily limits me in discussing what is inaccurately called the Judgment. I do not indeed admit the doctrine which has been advanced, that the Clergy in general are forbidden by the Oath of Supremacy to discuss the reasons of the Committee of Privy Council for the advice it has tendered to the Crown. Those who take this view are perhaps unaware that the Judgment (so-called) which has excited so much discussion, is an entirely different document from the Report to the Crown, upon which the real Judgment is founded; that the so-called Judgment is a state-

B 2

ment for the guidance of the suitors and the public of the grounds upon which the advice to the Crown will be based, which statement never reaches the Crown at all; and that the Report to the Crown happily omits the grounds of the advice, and confines itself to advising briefly what the Judgment should be.* By this course the great inconvenience is prevented that reasons which must of necessity be closely and freely criticised in arguing new cases as they arise, would appear as part of the Judgment of the Queen, and that the mind of the Advocate would thus be divided between his respect for the Sovereign and his duty to his client. The Clergy are happily

---

* The Report and Judgment in one of the Cases is annexed :—

"'Now the Lords of the Committee having, in obedience to your Majesty's said Order in Council, taken the said Petition into consideration, and read the proceedings transmitted from the Court below, and on three former days heard the said Appellant and his Proctor and Counsel, and a Proctor for the Respondent, and having maturely deliberated, have this day agreed humbly to report to your Majesty their opinion in favour of the Appeal and Complaint of the said Reverend Rowland Williams that the Decree or Sentence appealed from ought to be reversed ; that the Articles given in in the said Cause in the Court below by the Proctor of the said Right Reverend the Lord Bishop of Salisbury, and which were by the said Judge admitted as reformed, ought to be rejected; and that the said Reverend Rowland Williams, clerk, the Appellant, ought to be dismissed from the Decree or Citation against him issued under seal of the Court below pursuant to the Letters of Request, in virtue of which the said Cause was promoted, and from all further observance of justice in the said Cause ; and, further, that the said Right Reverend the Lord Bishop of Salisbury, the Respondent, ought to be condemned in the costs incurred by the said Appellant in the said Cause of Appeal, but that no order ought to be made in regard to the costs incurred on either side in the said Cause in the Court below.'

"Her Majesty, having taken the said Report into consideration, was pleased, by and with the advice of her Privy Council, to approve thereof, and of what is therein recommended, and to order, as it is hereby ordered, that the same be duly and punctually observed, complied with, and carried into execution. Whereof all persons whom it may concern are to take notice, and govern themselves accordingly."

not placed under that intolerable restraint, that a
number of theological statements, drawn up in fact
by a Committee with a majority of eminent laymen,
and partly repudiated by two out of the three pro-
fessed theologians that compose the minority, are removed from the sphere of theological discussion and
placed under the protection of the Oath of Supremacy.
If a Committee of the Privy Council of the Queen
imparts to the suitors and to the public the grounds
of the advice it means to tender, the public and the
suitors will form an opinion as to whether Her
Majesty is likely to be rightly or wrongly advised.
And whilst the Oath of Supremacy binds us to regard
the Judgment of the Crown as final and decisive
between the parties, it does not impose on the Clergy
the distasteful duty of imputing to the Crown pro-
positions or reasoning which their own studies
enable them to recognise as defective, which may
happen to be corrected in some future case, which
emanate not from the Crown but from responsible
servants of Her Majesty, and which are not even
submitted to the Crown after being delivered to the
public.

But the liberty which I thus claim for the Clergy
and for all others, I can only exercise with those
restrictions which attach to a member of the Court.
I cannot reopen the whole case and compare the
Judgment with the pleadings and with the facts in
evidence. I shall pass no opinion on the Judgment
of the Arches Court, which has now been reviewed by
the Privy Council. But in the discharge of my spi-
ritual office I am bound to speak upon those theolo-

gical topics as to which the minds of Christian people are from any cause disquieted, and to point out what is the effect of the "Judgment" upon the position of the Church.

It is important to observe that a much wider scope is attributed to the "Judgment" than it claims for itself. The course of proceeding in the Court of Arches recognises a twofold right of appeal. Either party may appeal, either on the admission of the articles of charge or on the judgment being pronounced. An appeal at the former of these two stages would have raised the question, What passages in the "Essays" impugned are heretical? An appeal at the latter stage is confined to the much narrower question, Do certain quoted passages deserve, as heretical, the penalty decreed by the Court below? Now the appeal to the Privy Council was in this narrower form ; it was an appeal against the judgment of the Court of Arches, and not against its order for the reformation of the articles of charge. It was an appeal against the penalty, and not an appeal upon the whole merits of the cases. If the Judge of the Court of Arches was wrong in admitting or rejecting any passages as heretical, either party could have appealed, and so the opinion of the Privy Council would have been obtained as to the whole case, as to what passages in the whole Essay were, and what were not, at variance with our articles and formularies. If the promoter thought that after the large changes directed by the Judge to be made in the articles of charge the quotations still admitted would give a wrong idea of the unsound teaching of the defendant, he might have had his remedy with the Court above, and might have there resisted the omissions and alterations ordered by the Judge of the Arches. But in each case the promoter waived that right of appeal; and neither case came to the Court above until the later stage—the appeal against the punishment.

I purposely refrain from expressing any opinion as to the judgment of the Court below, because this is beyond the limit I have imposed on myself. I only say that, whatever may be thought of that judgment upon the admission of the articles, the promoters rested content with it, and thus narrowed the ground which the Committee of Council were permitted to travel over. And it follows that the Committee of Council has pronounced no opinion whatever upon the "Essays" of the two defendants, but only upon some detached fragments of them.

Nor can it be regarded as an injury to the faith of the Church that the Committee of Council has imposed on itself the strictest bounds in dealing with these fragments. "The accuser is, for the purpose of the charge, confined to the passages which are included and set out in the Articles as the matter of the accusation; but it is competent to the accused party to explain from the rest of his work the sense or meaning of any passage or word that is challenged by the accuser." We may infer from these words that the Court will not have regard to any other portion of the work in which the passages occur; but that if the accused resorts to other parts of his work to explain away the accusation, the accuser may follow him into the same ground to refute the explanation. But if after the parties have been heard, without having travelled beyond the passage, a doubt shall exist in the mind of the Court whether the passage in question be heretical, or be devoid of all sense and meaning, the Court is not to cast even a glance into the rest of the work in order to clothe it with meaning; but is bound, if it be not clearly heretical in itself, rather to consider it as unmeaning altogether. This strict rule may narrow the functions of the Court unduly, and may be at variance with the practice of other Courts in the analogous case of a libel; but there is no peril to the faith of the Church where a passage escapes censure because the Court cannot see its meaning, and declines to seek assistance elsewhere.

These remarks seem necessary, because, in spite of the explicit disclaimer in the " Judgment," many persist in treating it as an examination and acquittal of the whole work called " Essays and Reviews."

There are only two points in the " Judgment" to which these remarks do not apply, and about which after all these limitations the mind of the Church is reasonably disquieted. I mean the inspiration and authority of Holy Scripture, and the eternity of the punishment of the wicked.

Upon the former of these points, the authority of Scripture, I must not shrink from saying that a doctrine as to Holy Scripture has found some countenance from the " Judgment," which no article or formulary of any Church whatever has before adopted, namely : That the Bible is called the Word of God, not because it is, but because it contains the Word of God.

One of the Appellants maintains that the title "Word of God" cannot properly be applied to the whole Bible by Protestants, because it is not so applied in the Bible itself, and Protestants own no other authority than the Bible. He thinks that the doctrine of the Church on this subject is to be sought for in the Sixth Article, which he terms the "pivot article," and this doctrine he thus expresses: "The Word of God is contained in Scripture, whence it does not follow that it is co-extensive with it."

The other Appellant maintains, in two passages that are certainly not free from obscurity, that the Bible is the production of devout human beings, which other devout human beings are entitled to criticise freely; that seeing the Prayer Book speaks of the Church as inspired, we ought not to shrink from attributing inspiration to "true hearts" in all ages merely because they are fallible, but we ought rather to reduce our theory of the inspiration of prophets and apostles to the same level, and confess that those "Israelites of old" might be fallible also, and that the inspiration which guided the writers of the Bible is the same in kind as that which Luther and Milton and other good men have at different times enjoyed.

Obscure as the words of this writer are, I assume that they have a meaning, and this is the only meaning which I am able to attach to them.

One Appellant then maintains that the Bible is not the Word of God, and the other that it is the word of devout men. These two doctrines are opposed not merely to one or more statements of our Church, but to those statements which are the very foundation of its teaching.

The doctrine of the Church on this subject is set forth in the 6th and 20th Articles principally, but several other Articles contain expressions bearing on the subject, as the 19th, 21st, 22nd, 24th, and 26th. Not one of these Articles is directed against those who deny the authority of Scripture, but the doctrine is gathered from the expressions used about the Bible in guarding against errors of a different kind.

The 6th Article is directed against those who hold that traditions are necessary besides Scripture. The word "containeth" does not imply that any part of Scripture is less inspired, less canonical than another; the assertion is that all things necessary to salvation are found in Holy Scripture. They are contained, but not as the less in the greater, not as one part in a whole, but as all the parts together are contained in the whole which they constitute. The latter part of the Article enumerating the Books of Scripture introduces the well-known distinction between canonical and apocryphal books. It has been argued that there are two senses of the word *canonical*, but this is not admissible. I do not believe that that sense of canonical, as "admitted into a list or index of works to be used in public worship," was in the mind of those who drew up the Articles at all. It originated, I think, with Semler in Germany, but it is now quite exploded, even among those who more or less follow Semler's opinions. There is every reason to think, and no reason on the other side, that in the Article the word canonical has its proper historical meaning. Originally the canon was the rule of faith in the Church ; then as Holy Scripture came everywhere to be accepted as the rule of faith, the Bible was called " the canon of Holy Scriptures " by Chrysostom, " the canonical Scriptures " by Origen, " canonized books " by Chrysostom, always with the sense that, as divine writings, they were the norm and rule of the faith. The word canonical means in the 6th Article " belonging to the rule of faith." Books could not be canonical, could not guide and regulate and determine the faith, unless they were divine.

The Bible is termed the Word of God in the 19th, 20th, 22nd, and 24th Articles. None of these Articles was drawn up with reference to those who deny divine authority to the Bible; but this error, though not present to the mind of the framers of the Articles, receives indirectly a sufficient refutation from the passages that can be cited.

In Article 22 Scripture and the Word of God are treated as interchangeable terms.

In Article 20 a very important statement occurs : " And yet it is not lawful for the Church to ordain anything that is contrary to God's Word written, neither may it so expound one place of Scripture that it be repugnant to another." Here Holy Scripture is made the judge of controversies, or rather, as it has been said, the voice of the judge ; and a limit is put to the right of interpreting a passage " according to the mind of the Church " claimed by some Romish writers, by the rule that one place of Scripture is not to be interpreted against another. Nothing can more clearly show the sense which the Church puts upon the phrase "Word of God." If no text is to be interpreted against another, this must be because all the Bible is regarded as divine and canonical.

Besides these passages, there is the question put to every one to be ordained Deacon: "Do you unfeignedly believe all the Canonical Scriptures of the Old and New Testament?" with the answer, "I do believe them." *

How stands the case, then, with the Appellants? One of them has affirmed that the Bible cannot properly be called by us the Word of God, though it is so called in the 20th and other Articles; and has maintained that the Word of God is something contained in Scripture but not co-extensive with it, which is contrary to the 6th and 20th Articles, and to the profession of unfeigned belief in all the Canonical Scriptures of the Old and New Testament, made by every one who is ordained Deacon.

---

* Were it necessary to show that other Protestant communities have spoken of the Bible as the Word of God, the task would be easy. In the Preface to the Augsburg Confession (p. 6) the teaching of the Reformers is described as drawn "ex Scripturis Sanctis et puro verbo Dei," the two expressions being synonymous. In the 'Apology for the Confession' (p. 48) the adversaries of the Lutherans are described as condemning doctrines in defiance of the Scripture of the Holy Spirit (" contra manifestam Scripturam Spiritûs Sancti"). In the Smalcaldic Articles (p. 308) it is written, "We have another rule, namely, that the Word of God may establish Articles of Faith, and no one besides, not even an angel." And these Articles (pp. 331-333) describe a class of enthusiasts who profess that "they have the Spirit before the Word and without the Word, and therefore judge, and turn, and twist the Scripture, or the vocal Word" [elsewhere "the external-Word"] "at their pleasure." In the 'Formula Concordiæ' Luther is described as laying down clearly this difference between Divine and human writings, "Solas videlicet Sacras literas pro unica regula et norma omnium dogmatum cognoscendas." All these passages will be found in Francke's 'Libri Symbolici Eccl. Luther.'

The other Appellant contends that the Bible is the production of devout human beings, which other devout human beings may freely criticise; that the inspiration which guided it is the same in kind as that which Luther and Milton and other good men have at different times enjoyed. This is in contradiction of the 6th Article, which attributes canonical authority to the books of Holy Writ; to the 20th Article, which forbids the Church to ordain anything contrary to God's word written, or to expound one place of Scripture so that it be repugnant to another. The infallibility of Scripture is here plainly taught: the Appellant advisedly contends for the fallibility.

I had no doubt that both Appellants were clearly shown, even under the narrow rule laid down by the Committee of Council, to have broken the law of the Church, and to have advisedly taught what was contrary to the doctrines of the Church in her articles and formularies. Being unable to concur in the advice to be given to the Crown, the two Primates recorded their dissent from this portion of the judgment.

It is almost superfluous to observe that this is no question of terms but of doctrine, and that it is not a question of one doctrine but of the doctrine on which all the other doctrines of the Church of England rest. It is a question of the binding authority of Holy Scripture. In pronouncing the Bible to be the Word of God, in taking from all Deacons a pledge of belief as to all the books of the Bible, in calling the books of the Old and New Testaments canonical, in declaring that Holy Scripture contains all things necessary to salvation, in prohibiting inconsistent or contrary interpretations of Scripture, the Church of England expresses with sufficient clearness that God has spoken to His people the word of His will so that all can understand it and use it for their guidance, that the Bible is this word, and that its teaching, which cannot contradict itself, is the law, or norm, or canon, by which the Church is bound. The Church has laid down no theory of inspiration; she has always had in her bosom teachers of at least two different theories. But she does lay down that the declarations of Scripture are intelligible, are self-consistent, are of supreme authority. If the Bible is not the Word of God, but contains the Word of God as the greater contains the less, every one of these predicates falls to the ground. There is no touchstone which shall test for us whether a given passage is part of the Word of God or of the word of man therewith entangled; and so we can no longer depend on understanding the will of God from the Bible. Passages may admit of a contrary interpretation if some are and some are not of divine origin; and therefore the Bible would cease to be self-consistent. And that book can no longer be of supreme authority in controversies of faith; we should either be without an authority, from our inability to discern and disentangle the divine and human portions, or the supreme authority would be that power which claimed to teach us what was divine and what was human.

Thus far as to the statements of one Appellant. Those of the other tend as directly towards the same result. If those " Israelites of old," whom we term prophets and apostles, are fallible writers, and their works to be classed only with devout human compositions, we have no right to expect from them a clear, or an uniformly consistent, or an authoritative decision.

What then are we to teach ? Where is " the very lively Word of God, the special food of man's soul, that all Christian persons are bound to embrace, believe, and follow, if they look to be saved?"* The Church of England answers that the Bible is that Word. The new doctrine seems to leave us without an answer.

And whilst I have exactly adhered to the rule laid down by the legal members of the Committee that the passages inculpated were to be interpreted by themselves, and that the Court could not seek for itself any illustration of them even from the writer's own words in the same Essay, I must point out the serious consequences of deciding theological doctrines upon such a basis, both as regards the suitors, and as regards the Church.

As regards the suitors, these proceedings are highly penal, and penalties almost always involve questions of degree. When a writer denies that the whole Bible is the Word of God, the statement is in terms contradictory to those of our Church. But as to the punishment, it makes the greatest difference —the difference between a venial want of caution in the use of words, and a highly culpable error— whether the writer means to exclude on critical

---

* Injunctions of King Edward VI.

grounds a few verses which ought not to be considered parts of the Bible, or wishes to shut out all miracle, and 'all 'prediction, and much of the sacred history. Now in one of the cases before us a writer has asserted that no one can call the Bible the Word of God, and has then proceeded to show with sufficient openness many special places of Scripture to which his principle applies. The passage is one continuous whole; and cannot be divided with justice to the author's meaning. If an author states a general principle and thinks fit to add the particulars to which it applies, he has a right to ask that both the one and the other shall be looked on as essential to his argument. The Committee of Council by its rule is precluded from looking at any thing which the Court below has struck out; the Court below has struck out all examples taken from Holy Scripture; so that the universal proposition is stated, but the examples which show the amount of its application are all excluded.

It is obvious to answer that the Appellant has been acquitted, and so needs not complain. But there are two parties to a suit. The Promoter has thought it right to obtain the opinion of the Courts upon this passage. The Court of Arches decides that half of it must be struck out, and that the remaining half is highly penal. The Privy Council determines that the remaining half is not penal at all; but guards itself against any decision, except as to that half. Neither tribunal will have anything to do with the whole passage. The Promoter is unable to read it except as a whole,—perhaps could not foresee that it would be read otherwise. The Promoter gets no substantial answer, but pays the costs.

As regards the Church, which has all along watched these cases with great anxiety, the results of the operation of this rule are equally unsatisfactory. The Promoter had at least the choice of two appeals; the Church could only wait. The Church expected an interpretation of the law upon this passage from the proper Courts. The result of the whole proceeding is that it receives an opinion upon half the passage : upon the abstract assertion and not upon the concrete illustrations of it. Nay, what is more surprising, the author's own examples being lost in the Court below, fresh ones are supplied him, and the sense of the passage is thus completely transformed. The Council tries the question whether it is heretical to " affirm that any part of the canonical books of the Old or New Testament, *upon any subject whatever, however unconnected with religious faith or moral duty*, was not written under the inspiration of the Holy Spirit ? " Are we then to infer from the acquittal that the author's own examples, " the nature of angels, the reality of demoniacal possession, the personality of Satan, and *the miraculous particulars of many events*," are determined by the Committee to be " matters unconnected with religious faith or moral duty ? " By no means. The Court below has deprived the Committee of the benefit of the author's own examples; and they have applied his principles to particulars of their own, to " matters unconnected with religious faith and moral duty." For no other reader, beyond the doors of the

Council Chamber, can this half passage be said to have any existence. No other reader will stop in the middle of the page lest he should see how the author developes his own meaning. No other reader would discard the author's own examples and put in others of his own. What must be the result? The Council speaks of one thing, and the author perhaps of another; but the words of the Council will be applied to the passage as it stands, which alone has any existence as a ground for the charge.

Unlearned persons know but two ways of dealing with an incomplete statement; it may either be left unexplained as incomplete, or the author's own words may be called in to complete it.

The charge against one Appellant on the subject of Eternal Punishment did not seem to me to be sustained. On the one hand the Church in adopting the word everlasting to express the word that may also be rendered eternal, has cut off, for all purposes of law, some metaphysical speculations to which the original word has been subjected. Everlasting must mean lasting for ever, never coming to an end. The Church of England believes in a life that lasts for ever for the good, and in an everlasting punishment of the wicked.

But on the other hand, the Appellant explained to the Court that the "all" of whom he predicated salvation at the last, did not include all men without exception; that he divided men into three classes —the utterly reprobate, the good, and a middle class of undeveloped or "germinal souls;" and that it was this middle class, whose characters at the hour of

death did not mark them either as good or bad, of
whom he hoped that they might hereafter be developed
into something higher, and might be made fit for
the bosom of the Father. Although this was not a
formal retractation of anything he had advanced,
yet as the words employed would bear that construction, with a little allowance for incautious writing,
it did not seem to be right to inflict a heavy penalty
for maintaining that all would be saved, in the face
of a declaration that he meant "all the good and all
the undeveloped," to the exclusion of the reprobate.
The charge fell to the ground if the writer's own
explanation was to be taken.

. It must be remembered that our duty was to deal
with *advised* teaching contrary to the articles and
formularies.

As the Appellant did not directly impugn the formularies where they speak of this subject; as he
expressed no more than a hope or wish; above all,
as he insisted that his words had been overstrained
beyond their meaning, I felt justified in agreeing in
the opinion that he had not been guilty of advised
teaching that had incurred the penalty awarded by
the Court below.

The "Judgment" omits the consideration that had
most weight with me, namely, the author's own explanation of his words, and, therefore, I could not
adopt all its expressions. Let me, however, point out
to some who have considered them as equivalent to an
admission that "the Church of England has left the
eternity of punishment an open question," that this
is by no means the construction that can be fairly

put upon them : " We do not find in the formularies to which this article refers any such distinct declaration of our Church upon the subject, *as to condemn as penal the expression of a hope* by a clergyman that even the ultimate pardon of the wicked who are condemned in the Day of Judgment may be consistent with the will of Almighty God." Our Church should not be too ready to make a hope or wish the ground of a criminal proceeding ; but it does not follow that the hope or wish is in conformity to the teaching of the Church because it is left to reason and argument and is not punished.

The doctrine of a terminable punishment for the wicked finds no countenance whatever from Holy Scripture. Those who have maintained it can do no more than suggest plausible explanations of texts that make against them ; even they must admit that there is not one passage of Scripture that clearly authorises the hope of universal salvation. On the other hand the declarations that the punishment of the wicked is eternal are many, and those most clear and emphatic. Eternal death put into antithesis with eternal life ; eternal chains ; the wrath of God abiding on a man so that he shall never see life ; the worm that never dieth ; can all these be explained away ? Even if they could, not one of them promises salvation for the sinner once condemned. If they were not conclusive for everlastingness, they would not be in favour of the salvation of the wicked at the last. On the other hand, the doctrine that the wicked are punished for ever would be gathered not from these express texts alone, but from the whole tenor of Scripture, which speaks of this life as our probation and of the next as our reward, which represents the judgment as final; which is utterly silent as to any economy of probation after death. I beseech my brethren of the clergy to beware of exceeding or departing from the statements of Scripture upon this awful subject. We are in the hands of a just God, who has revealed in Holy Writ His way of dealing with His creatures so far as we need to know it for a guide to our faith and a motive to practical duties. Let us rest in that revelation. The certain consequence of attempting to make another doctrine, not in Scripture, of death and judgment, heaven and hell, will be to disturb the faith of our people in the plain declarations of the Bible, and to give them instead some fine-spun metaphysical view of evil, which their practical sense will soon detect as unwarranted by the voice of inspiration. I do not impute to this Appellant the intention to leave his people without definite belief in the future state. But if we destroy where we cannot rebuild, this will be the consequence. If the Bible statements be removed, who will pretend to interpret for us the secret things that lie behind the grave? The new speculation that some one gives us instead, may satisfy its author, may be honestly deemed by him an act of service to the Most High. But the strength of sin no cords of man's invention can bind; the wicked will break through such theories, as the strong man brake the green withes, " as a thread of tow is broken when it toucheth the fire," and sinners, bound now neither by Scripture nor by the weak cords of man's spinning, will draw their own conclusion, " We shall not surely die."

I have now touched upon the two great questions which have troubled men's minds : the authority of the Bible, and the punishment of the impenitent sinner. It would be vain to deny that this trouble of the Church has a real foundation. And yet, my brethren, there is no reason for immoderate fear. The Church of England depends for her teaching not upon prosecutions and decisions of Courts, but upon the solemn undertaking, freely made by her ministers, that they will teach the people according to her articles and formularies. In her articles the paramount authority of Holy Writ is to my mind sufficiently established. The Clergy will not subscribe the articles and teach out of the Prayer Book, without feeling and declaring to the people that the Bible is for us the law of the Church and the voice of God. From our northern province not one single case of doctrine has gone up to the Court of Appeal since that Court received its present constitution. It may be, that many now fear that the advice given to the Queen might not in some future case be in harmony with the conclusions of the great mass of the Clergy. Still it is not to be thought that our teachers have up to this time been kept straight by the fear of a tribunal, which in fact we have never used. If one of us should be tempted to err from the faith, more powerful than such a fear will be the common sense of his people, who with the Bible in their hands, and the Prayer Book that acknowledges the Bible, will refuse to be led off from its plain statements; more powerful will be the voice of his own conscience that tells him what he has freely undertaken to teach, and how far he may depart from it without ceasing to be a teacher in a Church that is founded on the Bible. The Church of England knows little of courts and prosecutions; and her stability and soundness in the faith rest upon a different and a far surer guarantee.

May our present perplexity make the ministers more zealous in teaching the pure Word of God, and the people more ready to hear and obey the same Word. Already great zeal for this precious heritage of the Church has been called forth. And though clouds and darkness are round us, they do not wholly obscure the wider horizon; and we know that He who has brought the pure Gospel to us in safety through past ages of trouble, is able to preserve it to us for the time to come.

(Signed)   W. EBOR:

PRIMATE OF ENGLAND AND METROPOLITAN.

April, 1864.

LONDON:

PRINTED BY WILLIAM CLOWES AND SONS, STAMFORD STREET,
AND CHARING CROSS.

A

CHARGE

TO THE CLERGY AND CHURCHWARDENS

OF THE

DIOCESE OF SALISBURY,

AT HIS TRIENNIAL VISITATION,

IN AUGUST, 1864.

BY WALTER KERR,

BISHOP OF SALISBURY.

SALISBURY:
BROWN AND CO, CANAL.
LONDON: RIVINGTONS. OXFORD· PARKER

Brethren, dear brethren, in a common work of faith and love, may such thoughts quicken every heart among us. May we all love to speak more of the Coming One; may we preach Him with still deeper earnestness; may we still more frequently celebrate that feast of His love which is alike the witness and the prophecy of His return; may the watchword of the Apostolic Church be ours; may the 'Until He come' be the longed for limit of all labour, the blessed boundary of all care.

Thus living alway, as in our Master's presence here below, may we faithfully and bravely do His work, and when all is done, and He vouchsafes to call us home, may our works follow us. 'Behold, I come quickly, and my reward is with me to give every man according as his work shall be.'[1]

[1] Rev. xxii. 12.

Note A, p. 40.

The words of Lord Eldon are as follow:—'It has been uniformly said, especially as to marriages in London, that the Clergyman cannot possibly ascertain where the parties are resident: but that is an objection, which a Court, before whom the consideration of it may come, cannot hear. The Act of Parliament has given the means of making the enquiry, and if the means provided are not sufficient, it is not a valid excuse to the Clergyman, that he could not find out when the parties were resident, or either of them. If he has used the means given to him, and was misled, he is excusable; but he can never excuse himself if no enquiry was made.'

E. NEST, PRINTER, GLOUCESTER.

CPSIA information can be obtained
at www.ICGtesting.com
Printed in the USA
BVHW071307311218
536776BV00015B/2719/P

9 781332 612789